Child-Centered Math

Number Sense and Place Value

35 Hands-On Activities

Grades 2–3

Written by Cindy Barden and Gwen Botka
Edited by Janet Bruno
Illustrated by Terri Sopp Rae
Project Director: Carolea Williams

CTP ©1997, Creative Teaching Press, Inc., Cypress, CA 90630

Reproduction of activities in any manner for use in the classroom and not for commercial sale is permissible. Reproduction of these materials for an entire school or for a school system is strictly prohibited.

Table of Contents

To the Teacher i
Getting Started ii
About Number Sense and Place Value iii

Number Sense Activities

Number Hunt 1
Daily Numbers 2
By the Handful 3
About How Many? 4
Picture 100 5
Odd or Even? 6
Round It 7
Estimating Jar 8
How Close Can You Get? 9
Number Bingo 10
How Many Ways? 11
High Number Wins 12
Color It 13
Guess My Number 14
Exploring Area 15
Finding Fifty 16
Mystery Number 17
Answers Galore 18

Place Value Activities

Stamping Tens 19
Handful of Beans 20
Collecting Pennies 21
Show Me 22
Roll of the Dice 23
Three-Digit Combinations 24
Place Value Puzzles 25
Place Value Designs 26
Three Ways 27
Numbers to 999 28
I'm Full 29
Race to 50 30
Going to the Bank 31
Storytelling Math 32
Building Bigger Numbers 33
Chains of Ten 34
"X" Marks the Spot 35

Parent Letter 36
Hundred Chart 37
Place Value Board 38

To the Teacher

The child-centered activities in this book are the perfect way to enhance the development of good number sense and expand students' knowledge of place value. Each activity is quick to prepare and highly motivating, making learning about number sense and place value an enjoyable experience.

Number Sense and Place Value is designed as a handy resource for teachers, not a prescribed continuum of skills. Integrate the activities into your current mathematics program, keeping in mind the special needs of your students.

Have fun watching your students get excited about math as they participate in these hands-on activities.

Getting Started

Most activities can be implemented in small-or large-group settings, but some are best suited to learning centers where a few students can work independently. When planning the amount of adult guidance or participation needed, keep in mind the materials to be used, the type of work space needed, and the activity level of the project.

Number Sense and Place Value is ideal for involving teacher aides or parent volunteers in the classroom. The directions are simple and easy to follow, and students will quickly become engaged in the activities. It may be helpful to place a laminated copy of each activity in a box with the materials. This allows for instant setup and cleanup.

The suggested materials in *Number Sense and Place Value* are a combination of inexpensive, everyday objects and commonly-available commercial math manipulatives. As you review the materials lists, feel free to substitute materials as needed. A parent letter is included on page 36 to help you obtain various consumable materials.

About Number Sense

When students have number sense, they understand the relationships between numbers, are able to tell when an answer is reasonable, and can effectively use numbers in a variety of situations. Children with good number sense exhibit confidence in their answers and show a willingness to try new mathematical investigations. Number sense develops over many years. In fact, even adults continue to grow in this ability. So, you may see a wide disparity in skills and concepts among your second- and third-grade students.

About Place Value

Our base ten number system allows us to write any number using a selection or combination of just ten digits, because digits can have different values depending on their position in a number (e.g., 25 and 52). This is not always an easy concept for students to understand. To develop understanding, give students a variety of experiences counting, grouping, and trading objects to form tens, ones, hundreds, and so on. Students should also use place value manipulatives as they learn to compare larger numbers and add and subtract with regrouping.

Number Hunt

Activity 1

Materials

- old magazines, catalogs, newspapers
- scissors
- index cards
- glue
- chart paper
- markers

Procedure

1. Have students cut numbers and number words from magazines, catalogs, and newspapers and glue them on index cards.
2. Working with a small group, have students sort the cards by common attributes (e.g., fractions, ordinal numbers, decimals, times, numbers less than 100).
3. After all the cards are sorted, encourage students to sort by different attributes.
4. Make a list of the different attributes students use.

Extension Have students order the numbers from smallest to largest.

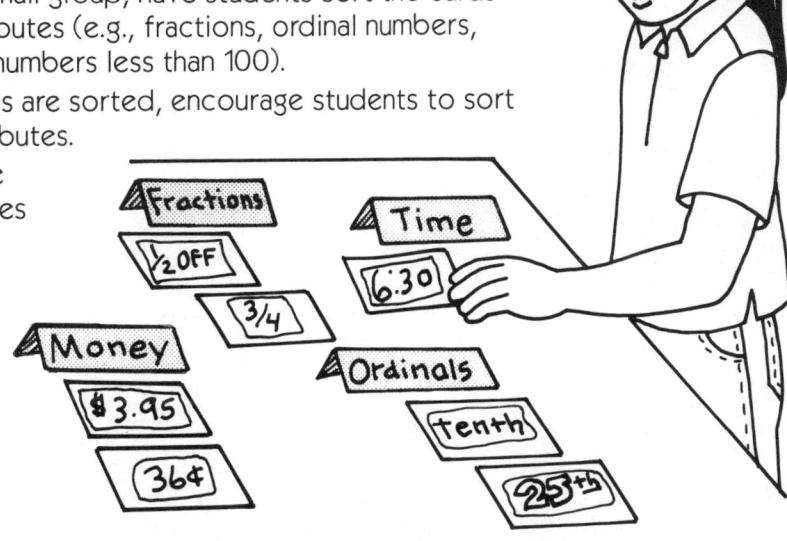

Number Sense and Place Value

Notes:

Extensions:

Daily Numbers

Activity 2

Materials
- math journals
- pencils
- drawing paper
- markers or crayons

Procedure
1. Every day for a week, ask students to record different ways they used numbers at home and at school.
2. Ask volunteers to read their journals and compare entries.
3. At the end of the week, have each student select one idea, write it down, and illustrate it.
4. Compile pages into a class book.

Notes:

Extensions:

By the Handful

Activity 3

Materials
- small objects
- bowl or bucket

Procedure
1. Working with a small group, invite each student to grab a handful of objects and count them.
2. Have students predict how many objects will be in two handfuls and verify their predictions.
3. Repeat with three handfuls.
4. Ask questions such as, "Was two handfuls double the number?" Was three handfuls triple?" "What was the most you were able to grab?"
5. Try this activity with different-sized objects.

Number Sense and Place Value

Notes:

Extensions:

About How Many?

Activity 4

Materials
- chalkboard
- chalk

Procedure

1. Working with a small group, ask one student to name an object in the room (e.g., chair).
2. Ask the rest of the group to estimate how many of those objects are in the room. Have them explain how they determined their estimates. For example, "I think there are about 30 chairs in the room because we have 25 students, plus the teacher's chair, plus a few extras at the work table."
3. Compare different students' estimates, allowing students to revise their estimates throughout the discussion.
4. Continue steps 1–3, giving each student several opportunities to name objects and estimate.

Number Sense and Place Value

Notes:

Extensions:

Picture 100

Activity 5

Materials
- flat toothpicks
- glue
- construction paper

Procedure
1. Have students make designs to show the value of 100 by gluing 100 toothpicks on construction paper.
2. Encourage them to use a pattern in their designs.
3. Post students' creations on a bulletin board entitled *Picture 100*.

Extension Have groups of ten students work together to make a design for 1,000.

Notes:

Extensions:

Odd or Even?

Activity 6

Materials
- linking cubes

Procedure
1. Give each student pair 30 linking cubes.
2. Say an even number less than 30, and ask students to build the number using two rows of cubes. For example, for the number *12*, partners can build two rows with six cubes each. There are no extra cubes because 12 is an even number.
3. Say an odd number less than 30, and ask students to build the number as described in step 2. For example, for the number *15*, partners can build two rows with seven cubes in each row. There will be one extra cube because 15 is an odd number.
4. Repeat with other numbers until students see the pattern for even and odd numbers.

Variation Have students build numbers by pairing up linking cubes. For example, six would have three pairs of cubes, but seven would have three pairs plus one.

Creative Teaching Press, Inc.   Number Sense and Place Value   6

Notes:

Extensions:

Round It

Activity 7

Materials
- 11 small cans
- craft sticks or tongue depressors
- markers

Procedure
1. Label the cans *0, 10, 20, 30, 40, 50, 60, 70, 80, 90, 100*. Write a random selection of numbers from 1–100 on craft sticks.
2. Work with a small group. Line up the cans in numerical order. Pass out several craft sticks to each student.
3. Have each student decide to which multiple of ten their numbers are closest (e.g., 78 is closest to 80, and 32 is closest to 30). Explain that numbers ending in five are rounded up.
4. Ask students to take turns placing their craft sticks in the correct cans. Have group members check each others' work.

Extension Label the cans *100–1,000* in multiples of 100. Write higher numbers on the craft sticks, and repeat the activity.

Notes:

Extensions:

Estimating Jar

Activity 8

Materials
- jar
- small objects

Procedure
1. Fill the bottom layer of a jar with one kind of object, such as nuts in the shell, linking cubes, or buttons.
2. Have students count the objects with you.
3. Ask them to estimate how many objects would fill the jar.
4. Fill the jar one-quarter full, counting as you go. Stop and let students revise their estimates.
5. Fill the jar half full, counting as you go. Stop again and let students revise their estimates.
6. Fill the jar to the top. Have students share their estimates and discuss their estimating strategies. Count the objects.
7. Repeat with other objects, or use jars of various shapes and sizes.

Notes:

Extensions:

How Close Can You Get?

Activity 9

Materials
- 3" x 5" index cards
- markers or crayons

Procedure
1. Have students work in groups of five to write numbers *1–100* on index cards.
2. Ask students to mix up the cards and place them face down in a loose pile (not a neat stack). Have each student take five cards.
3. Turn one card face up, and ask students to determine which of their cards is closest to the turned-up card. The student whose card is closest wins one card from each student and the turned-up card.
4. Tell each student to draw one new card and turn over a new card.
5. Play continues until not enough cards remain in the pile to play another round. The player with the most cards wins.

Number Sense and Place Value

Notes:

Extensions:

Number Bingo

Activity 10

Materials

- bingo game
- one 10-sided die (numbered 0–9)

Procedure

1. Give each student a bingo card. Select one student to call numbers.
2. Have the caller roll the die, and announce and record the number.
3. Students may cover any one number on their cards that contains the number called. For example, if a six is rolled, students can cover 6, 16, 26, 36, 46, 56, 60, 61, and so on. Encourage students to develop strategies to decide which numbers to cover.
4. Have the caller repeat step 2 until someone covers five numbers in a row—vertically, horizontally, or diagonally. The winner becomes the number caller for the next game.

Number Sense and Place Value

Notes:

Extensions:

How Many Ways?

Activity 11

Materials

- coins (pennies, nickels, dimes, quarters)
- paper
- rubber coin stamps
- stamp pads
- pencils

Procedure

1. Place materials at a center.
2. Ask students to use the coins to show different ways to make 10¢.
3. Have students record different coin combinations using coin stamps.
4. Have students do the same for 25¢, 50¢, and other values.

Extension Post a large sheet of butcher paper. Have students record different ways to make $1.00.

Number Sense and Place Value

Notes:

Extensions:

High Number Wins

Activity 12

Materials
- numbered dice
- chips (game pieces, buttons, pennies, counters)
- container
- paper
- pencils

Procedure
1. Divide the class into groups of three, and give each group three dice and ten game chips.
2. Have students take turns rolling the dice and arranging them to form the largest possible number. Ask students to record their numbers.
3. When all students have rolled the dice once, have them compare numbers to see which is the largest.
4. The student with the largest number takes one chip.
5. Play continues until all chips are gone. The player with the most chips wins.

Variation Have students make the smallest possible number with the dice.

Extension Use four dice and repeat the activity.

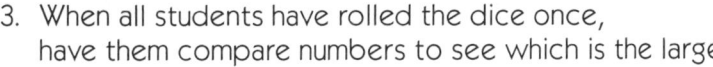

Number Sense and Place Value

Notes:

Extensions:

Color It

Activity 13

Materials
- index cards
- markers
- Hundred Chart reproducible (page 37)
- crayons

Procedure

1. Write directions similar to those below on index cards.
   - Color even numbers yellow.
   - Color odd numbers green.
   - Color numbers with the same digits blue.
   - Color multiples of three red.
   - Circle multiples of five, and place a box around multiples of four.
   - Color digits that differ by one.
2. Give each student pair an index card and two Hundred Charts.
3. Have students follow directions on their cards and compare results.
4. On another day, have students use a different card, or encourage them to look for patterns on their own cards.

Creative Teaching Press, Inc.

Number Sense and Place Value

Notes:

Extensions:

Guess My Number

Activity 14

Materials
- large hundred chart
- chalkboard
- chalk

Procedure
1. Play this game like Twenty Questions.
2. Post the hundred chart. Choose a student (the leader) to think of a number.
3. Have the rest of the class ask "yes" or "no" questions about the number. For example, "Is it less than 20?" "Is it an odd number?" "Is it between 50 and 70?"
4. As questions are answered, record clues as shown.
5. The goal is to guess the number in less than 20 questions. When the number is guessed, pick a new leader and play again.

Variation Have the leader mark off any numbers on the chart that the yes/no clues have eliminated.

Number Sense and Place Value

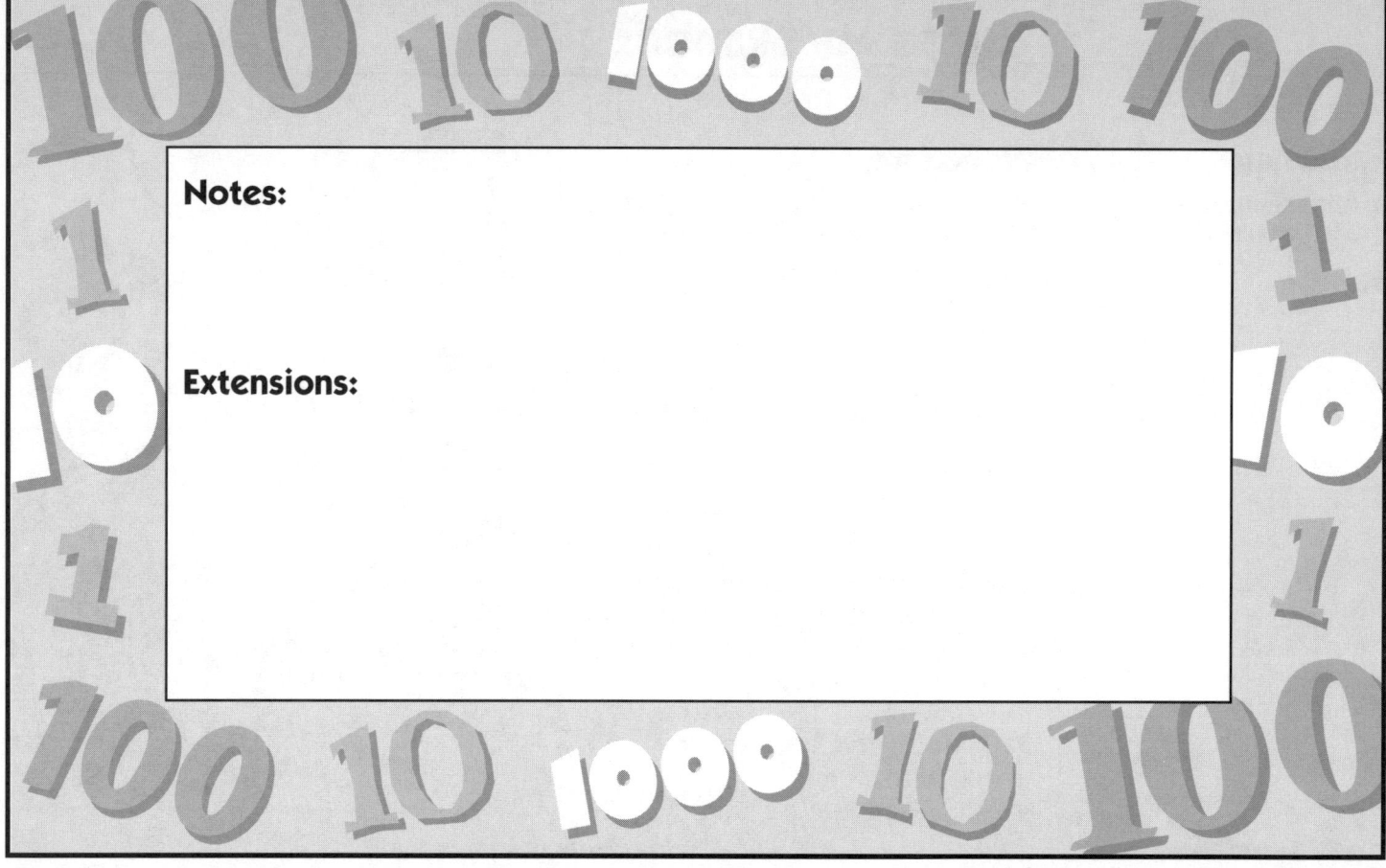

Notes:

Extensions:

Exploring Area

Activity 15

Materials
- different-sized books
- linking cubes, buttons, 1" paper squares
- paper
- pencils

Procedure
1. Give each student a book and some linking cubes, buttons, and paper squares.
2. Have students label a sheet of plain paper as shown.
3. Tell them to select one measuring unit (e.g., linking cubes), estimate how many it will take to completely cover their books, and record their estimates.
4. Ask students to cover the books with cubes, count, and record the number.
5. Have students repeat steps 3 and 4 with other measuring units.
6. Discuss their results. What unit gave you the largest/smallest number? Why?

Creative Teaching Press, Inc. Number Sense and Place Value

Notes:

Extensions:

Finding Fifty

Activity 16

Materials

- paper
- pencils
- counters or calculators
- chart paper
- markers

Procedure

1. Divide the class into small groups.
2. Ask students to write different ways to make 50 by adding (43 + 7), subtracting (62 - 12), multiplying (10 x 5), and dividing (100 ÷ 2). Have them record their equations. Encourage students to use counters or calculators to help them find different ways to make 50.
3. Make a chart as shown, recording each equation only one time.
4. On another day, repeat the activity with a different number.

Finding 50

+	−	×	÷
43+7	62-12	10×5	100÷2
25+25	100-50	25×2	
30+20	75-25		
25+20+5			

Notes:

Extensions:

Mystery Number

Activity 17

Materials
- chalkboard
- chalk
- large hundred chart
- paper
- pencils

Procedure
1. Write a number on a scrap of paper, but don't show the class. Post a large hundred chart so students can refer to it during the activity.
2. Write clues about the mystery number, one at a time, on the chalkboard. Start with general clues and then move to more specific ones.
3. After each clue, invite students to guess the mystery number.
4. When someone guesses the number, ask students to work in pairs to write clues for their own mystery numbers.
5. Each day, have one student pair present their clues, while the rest of the class uses good thinking strategies to guess the number.

Guess our mystery number.

Our Mystery Number — Ron
1. An even number less than 50.
2. A 2-digit number.
3. A factor of 36.
4. If you square the number, you get 144.

Number Sense and Place Value

Notes:

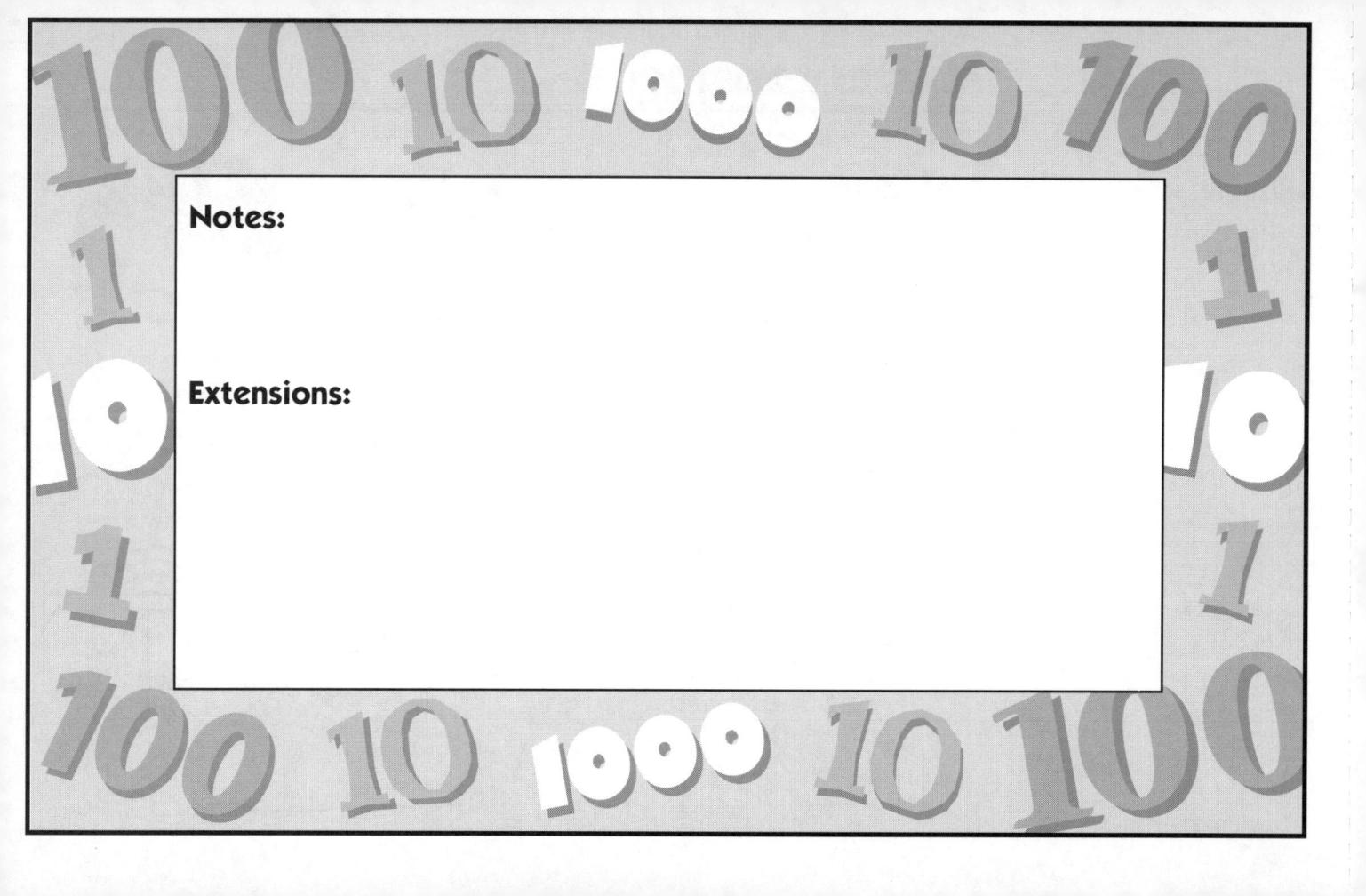

Extensions:

Answers Galore

Activity 18

Materials
- overhead projector
- transparency
- overhead markers
- paper
- pencils

Procedure
1. Write the answer to a math problem on the overhead. Use the format shown in the illustration. Choose problems appropriate for your class, and use any operation.
2. Have students work in pairs to complete the problem correctly.
3. After five or ten minutes, have volunteers write their solutions on the transparency.
4. Repeat the activity with other problems.

Creative Teaching Press, Inc.

Number Sense and Place Value

Notes:

Extensions:

Stamping Tens

Activity 19

Materials

- assorted small rubber stamps
- stamp pads
- 12" x 18" construction paper
- laminating supplies
- wipe-off markers

Procedure

1. Place materials at a center, and have each student print stamps all over a sheet of construction paper. Laminate the papers.
2. Encourage students to return to the center, select one paper, and use a wipe-off marker to circle stamps in groups of ten.
3. Have them write the total number on the paper, have a friend check it, and then erase the marker.

Extension Have students choose two papers and add up the total number on both sheets, grouping by tens.

Notes:

Extensions:

Handful of Beans

Activity 20

Materials
- dried beans
- small paper cups

Procedure
1. Give each pair of students some beans and cups.
2. Ask one student to grab a handful of beans, and have both partners estimate the amount of beans taken.
3. Tell students to check their estimates by counting the beans by tens into the cups.
4. Repeat the activity with two handfuls, three handfuls, and so on.

Variation Use cotton swabs and rubber bands for this activity. Secure the cotton swabs in bundles of ten with the rubber bands.

Notes:

Extensions:

Collecting Pennies

Activity 21

Materials
- pennies
- piggy bank
- coin wrappers

Procedure
1. Start a penny collection, and keep it going throughout the year.
2. As volunteers bring in pennies, put them in a piggy bank or money jar.
3. Each time the bank is full, have volunteers count the pennies by tens, then place 50 pennies in each coin wrapper to make 50¢.
4. Continue to add to the collection. At the end of the year, tally up the money saved and plan a class party.

Extension Each month have students record penny/dollar equivalents on a chart (e.g., *412 pennies = $4.12*).

Creative Teaching Press, Inc.

Number Sense and Place Value

Notes:

Extensions:

Show Me

Activity 22

Materials

- 8" straws, cut in half
- small rubber bands

Procedure

1. Divide the class into groups of three or four students. Have each group use rubber bands to make ten bundles of straws, with ten straws in each bundle. Provide extra single straws.
2. Ask one student in each group to name a number between 10 and 100. Have another student show that number using straw bundles and single straws. For example, if the first student says, *43,* the second student takes four bundles of ten straws and three single straws to show 43. Ask other group members to check his or her work.
3. Repeat the activity, giving each student several turns to say and show numbers.

Variation Use Base Ten Blocks for the activity and make four-digit numbers.

Notes:

Extensions:

Roll of the Dice

Activity 23

Materials
- dice
- Place Value Board reproducible (page 38)
- place value manipulatives
- paper
- pencils

Procedure
1. Divide the class into partners. Give each student pair two dice, two Place Value Boards, and manipulatives.
2. Tell Player A to roll the dice and make the largest number possible (e.g., for a two and six, 62 is the largest number).
3. Have Player A build the number with manipulatives on a Place Value Board.
4. Then, have Player B roll the dice and build a number.
5. Whoever builds the larger number wins one point. The player with the most points after ten rounds wins.

Extension Play with three or four dice and compare three- and four-digit numbers.

Notes:

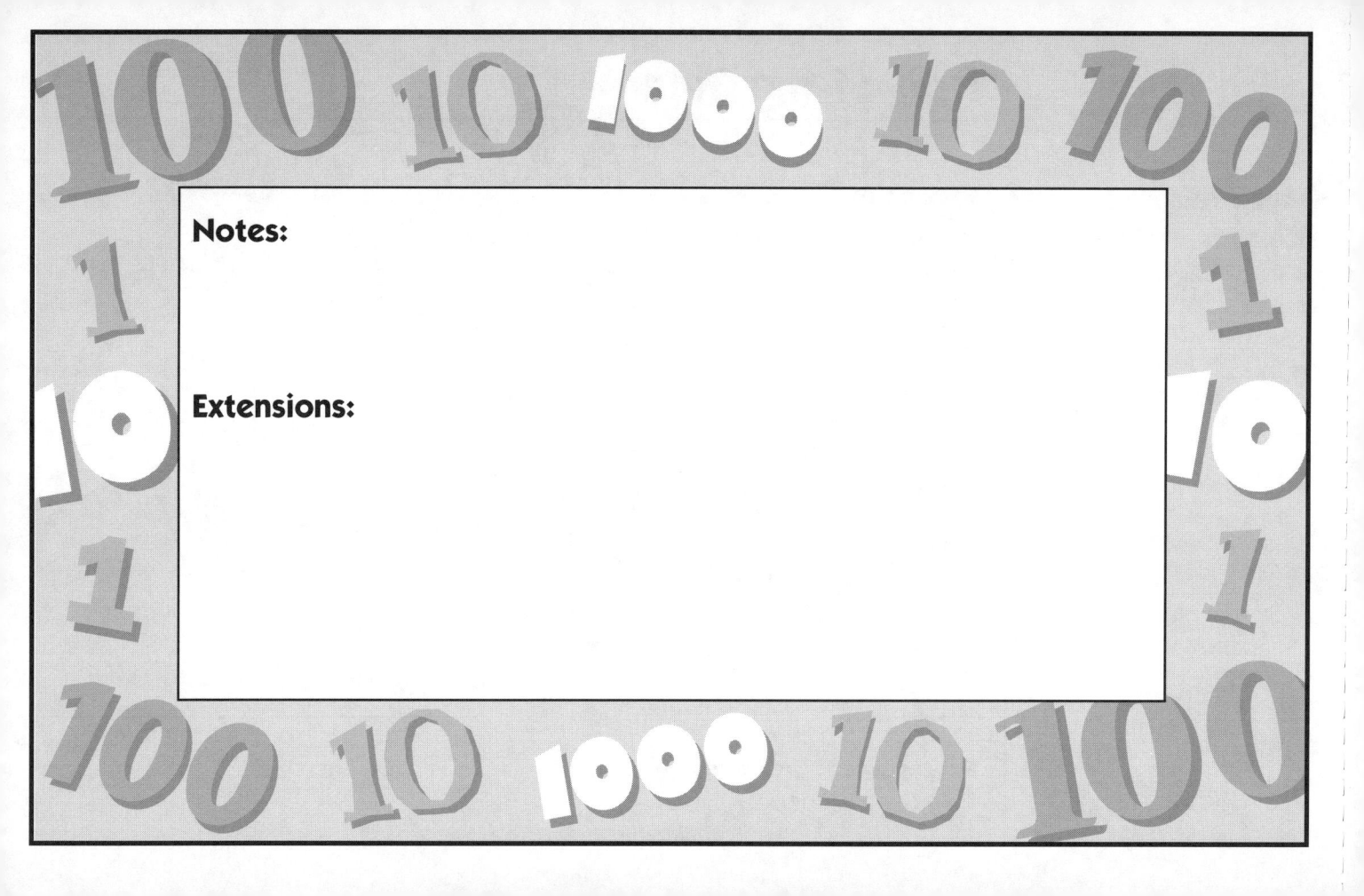

Extensions:

Three-Digit Combinations

Activity 24

Materials
- dice
- paper
- pencils

Procedure
1. Divide the class into small groups, and give each group three dice.
2. Ask one student in each group to roll the dice.
3. Have students write all possible three-digit numbers using the three numbers rolled. For example, if someone rolls three, six, and two, students write *236, 263, 326, 362, 623* and *632*.
4. Ask students to list the numbers in order from smallest to largest and compare lists to check their work.
5. Have students take turns repeating steps 2–4.

Extension Give each group four dice, and repeat the activity.

Number Sense and Place Value

Notes:

Extensions:

Place Value Puzzles

Activity 25

Materials

- transparency of Hundred Chart (page 37)
- overhead projector
- construction paper
- scissors

Procedure

1. Cut construction-paper puzzle shapes that fit over sections of the Hundred Chart transparency.
2. Place a puzzle shape on the transparency.
3. Ask students to use their knowledge of place value to name the numbers hidden by the shape. Have them explain how they figured out their answers.
4. Move the shape to another position, and ask students to name the new hidden numbers.
5. Repeat the activity using different puzzle shapes. Try using several shapes at one time.

Hundred Chart

1	2	3		5	6	7	8	9	10
11	12	13		15	16	17	18	19	20
21	22	23		25	26	27	28	29	30
31	32	33		35	36	37	38	39	40
41	42	43			46	47	48	49	50
51	52	53	54	55	56				
61	62	63	64	65	66		68	69	
71	72			75	76	77	78	79	80
81	82			85	86	87	88	89	90
91	92	93	94	95	96	97	98	99	100

Creative Teaching Press, Inc.

Number Sense and Place Value

Notes:

Extensions:

Place Value Designs

Activity 26

Materials
- construction paper (3 colors)
- paper cutter
- glue
- 12" x 18" drawing paper
- markers

Procedure
1. Cut large paper squares of one color for hundreds, strips of a second color for tens, and small squares of a third color for ones. Cut them to scale (e.g., the large square would be the same size as ten strips put together).
2. Have students make designs with the shapes and glue them on drawing paper.
3. Ask each student to write the number represented by his or her design.
4. Display designs on a bulletin board entitled *Place Value Designs*.

Creative Teaching Press, Inc.

Number Sense and Place Value

Notes:

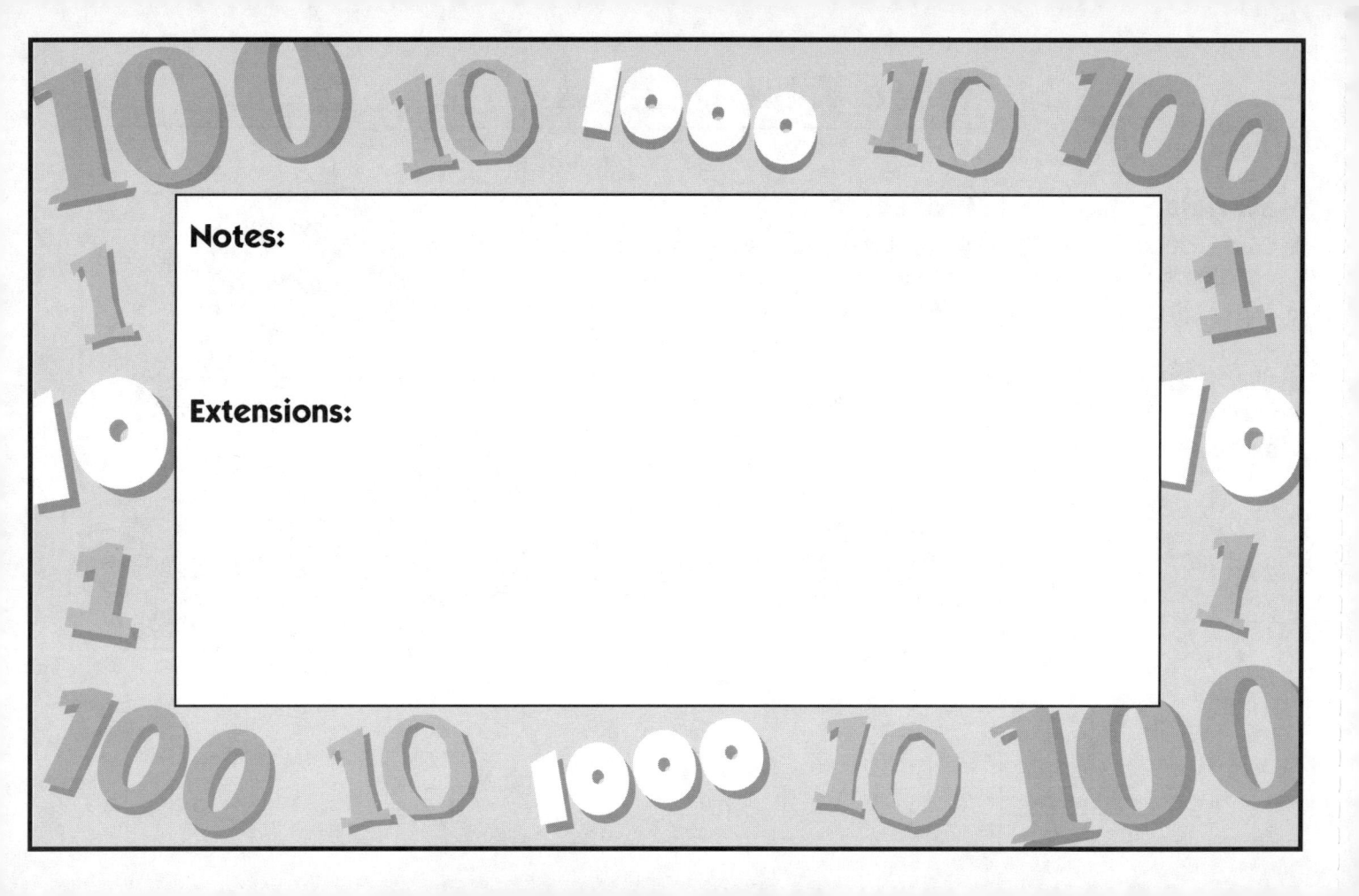

Extensions:

Three Ways

Activity 27

Materials
- Base Ten Blocks
- paper
- markers

Procedure

1. Divide the class into groups of three. Give each group Base Ten Blocks, paper, and markers.
2. Show students how to write a number in standard (361) and expanded (300 + 60 + 1) form.
3. Call out a number. Have one student in each group write the number in standard form. Have another student write the number in expanded form. Ask the third student to show it with Base Ten Blocks.
4. Call out other numbers, and have students take turns doing all three tasks.

Number Sense and Place Value

Notes:

Extensions:

Numbers to 999

Activity 28

Materials

- 1" graph paper
- red, blue, and white paper
- scissors
- markers
- paper
- pencils

Procedure

1. Reproduce a 1" graphing grid on red, blue, and white paper. Cut the blue paper into 3" x 1" cards, the red into 2" x 1" cards, and the white into 1" x 1" cards.
2. Have students make nine blue cards labeled *100–900* by hundreds, ten red cards labeled *00–90* by tens, and ten white cards labeled *0–9* by ones.
3. Tell students to select the following cards: *600, 40,* and *8.*
4. Show them how to overlap the cards to show *648.* Ask, "How many hundreds are there in 648? How many tens? How many ones?"
5. Ask them to write 648 in expanded form (600 + 40 + 8).
6. Continue with other numbers.

Extension To make four-digit numbers, add another color card for the thousands place.

Number Sense and Place Value

Notes:

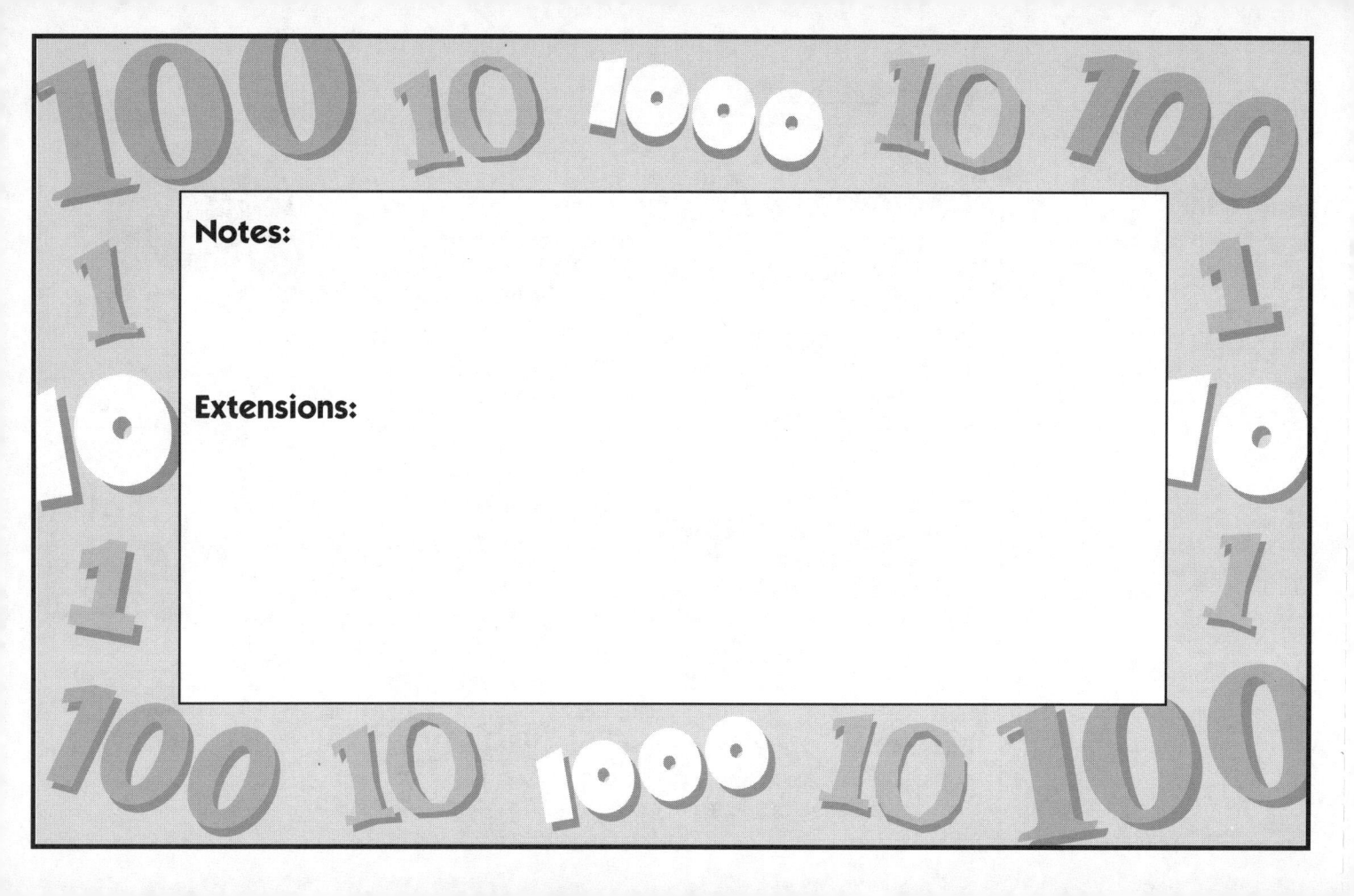

Extensions:

I'm Full

Activity 29

Materials

- small boxes of raisins
- Place Value Board reproducible (page 38)
- small paper cups
- dice

Procedure

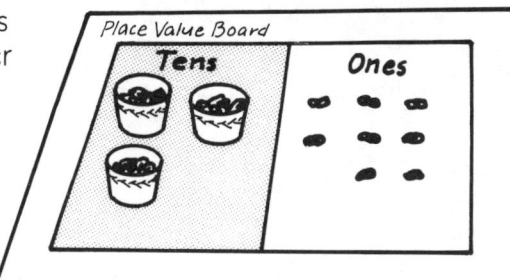

1. Working with a small group, give each student a die, box of raisins, and Place Value Board.
2. Ask students to pour out their raisins and count them. (Each group member should start with the same number of raisins. Even out numbers as needed.)
3. Have students begin with their Place Value Boards empty.
4. Tell each student to roll the die, and add that number of raisins to the board. When ten raisins are on the board, have students place them in a cup and place the cup on the tens section of the board.
5. Have students continue in this manner until one student has all of his or her raisins on the board.

Variation Have students start with all their raisins on the board and subtract the numbers rolled.

Number Sense and Place Value

Notes:

Extensions:

Race to 50

Activity 30

Materials

- linking cubes
- dice
- Place Value Board reproducible (page 38)

Procedure

1. Divide students into partners. Give each student a Place Value Board and linking cubes. Give each student pair one die.
2. Have students take turns rolling the die and using the cubes to build the number rolled.
3. Have students continue to add onto their cubes after each roll, regrouping ten ones into a ten when necessary.
4. The first student to reach 50 wins the game.

Extension Have each student use two dice and play to 100 or 200.

Notes:

Extensions:

Going to the Bank

Activity 31

Materials
- 6" x 18" paper
- markers
- dice
- "bank" (pennies, dimes, dollar bills)

Procedure
1. Working in small groups, give each student paper and a marker.
2. Have them fold the paper in three sections and label the columns *Dollars (hundreds), Dimes (tens),* and *Pennies (ones).*
3. Give each group a "bank" and a die. Ask one student to act as banker.
4. Have players take turns rolling the die and asking the banker for that amount of money in pennies. When a student has collected ten pennies, he or she trades them in to the bank for a dime. When a player has ten dimes, he or she trades them in for a dollar.
5. The first player to earn $1.00 wins.

Variation Use two dice and play to $5.00 or $10.00.

Number Sense and Place Value

Notes:

Extensions:

Storytelling Math

Activity 32

Materials

- Base Ten Blocks

Procedure

1. Work in groups of three to five students. Start by saying, "Twenty-eight birds sat on a branch. Show me this number."
2. Ask students to show the number of birds using Base Ten Blocks.
3. Then say, "Thirteen more birds landed on the branch. Show me how many birds there are now." Have students show the new number by adding the correct number of tens and ones, regrouping if necessary.
4. Ask a volunteer to make up a statement about how many birds flew away or landed.
5. Have students continue to add or subtract the correct number of tens and ones, regrouping if necessary, and continuing the story.
6. Start over using other situations (number of books in a reading center, blossoms in a garden, bees in a hive, and so on).

Notes:

Extensions:

Building Bigger Numbers

Activity 33

Materials

- place value manipulatives (hundreds, tens, ones)
- index cards
- markers
- chalkboard
- chalk

Procedure

1. Write the numbers *100, 200, 300, . . . 900* on index cards.
2. Have a small group of students sit in a circle.
3. Ask one student to select a number card and model the number with manipulatives.
4. Have the next student hold up a one, ten, or hundred model and say, "add one," "add ten," or "add 100" (e.g., "Jim started with 400. Now add 10 to 400").
5. Tell the next student to build the new number (410), and record it on the chalkboard.
6. Continue adding onto the original number until you've gone around the circle, then pick a new card and start again.

Creative Teaching Press, Inc.

Number Sense and Place Value

Notes:

Extensions:

Chains of Ten

Activity 34

Materials
- paper clips
- chalkboard
- chalk

Procedure
1. Have students work in small groups. Show them how to loop one paper clip through another to make a chain of ten paper clips. Ask them to make ten chains each. Also provide loose paper clips.
2. Write an addition or subtraction problem on the board.
3. Ask groups to use their paper clips to build the problem and do the indicated operation.
4. Tell each group to stand when they are done. The first group standing must explain how they got their answer. If correct, they get one point.
5. Play for a designated amount of time. The group with the most points wins.

Creative Teaching Press, Inc.

Number Sense and Place Value

Notes:

Extensions:

"X" Marks the Spot

Activity 35

Materials
- Hundred Chart reproducible (page 37)
- pencils

Procedure
1. Divide the class into small groups, and give each student a copy of the Hundred Chart.
2. Ask one student in each group to give directions, in tens and ones, to the rest of the group. For example, "Start at 96. Subtract six tens. Add two ones. Add one ten. What's the answer?"
3. When students find the number on their charts, have them mark it with an X.
4. Continue until all students in each group have had a chance to give directions.

Start at 96. Subtract six tens. Add two ones...

Creative Teaching Press, Inc.

Number Sense and Place Value

Notes:

Extensions:

Parent Letter

Dear Parents,

In our mathematics program, we are working on developing number sense and place value concepts. We will use a variety of materials and activities to make this unit fun and educational for students. If you would be willing to purchase an inexpensive, consumable item for these activities, please sign and return the bottom portion of this letter. I will then return the form to you stating the item and the date it is needed. Thank you!

Sincerely, _____

Yes, I would like to contribute an item for number sense and place value activities.

_____
(signature)

Please send in _____ by _____.
Thank you very much!

Hundred Chart

1	2	3	4	5	6	7	8	9	10
11	12	13	14	15	16	17	18	19	20
21	22	23	24	25	26	27	28	29	30
31	32	33	34	35	36	37	38	39	40
41	42	43	44	45	46	47	48	49	50
51	52	53	54	55	56	57	58	59	60
61	62	63	64	65	66	67	68	69	70
71	72	73	74	75	76	77	78	79	80
81	82	83	84	85	86	87	88	89	90
91	92	93	94	95	96	97	98	99	100

Number Sense and Place Value

Creative Teaching Press, Inc.

Place Value Board

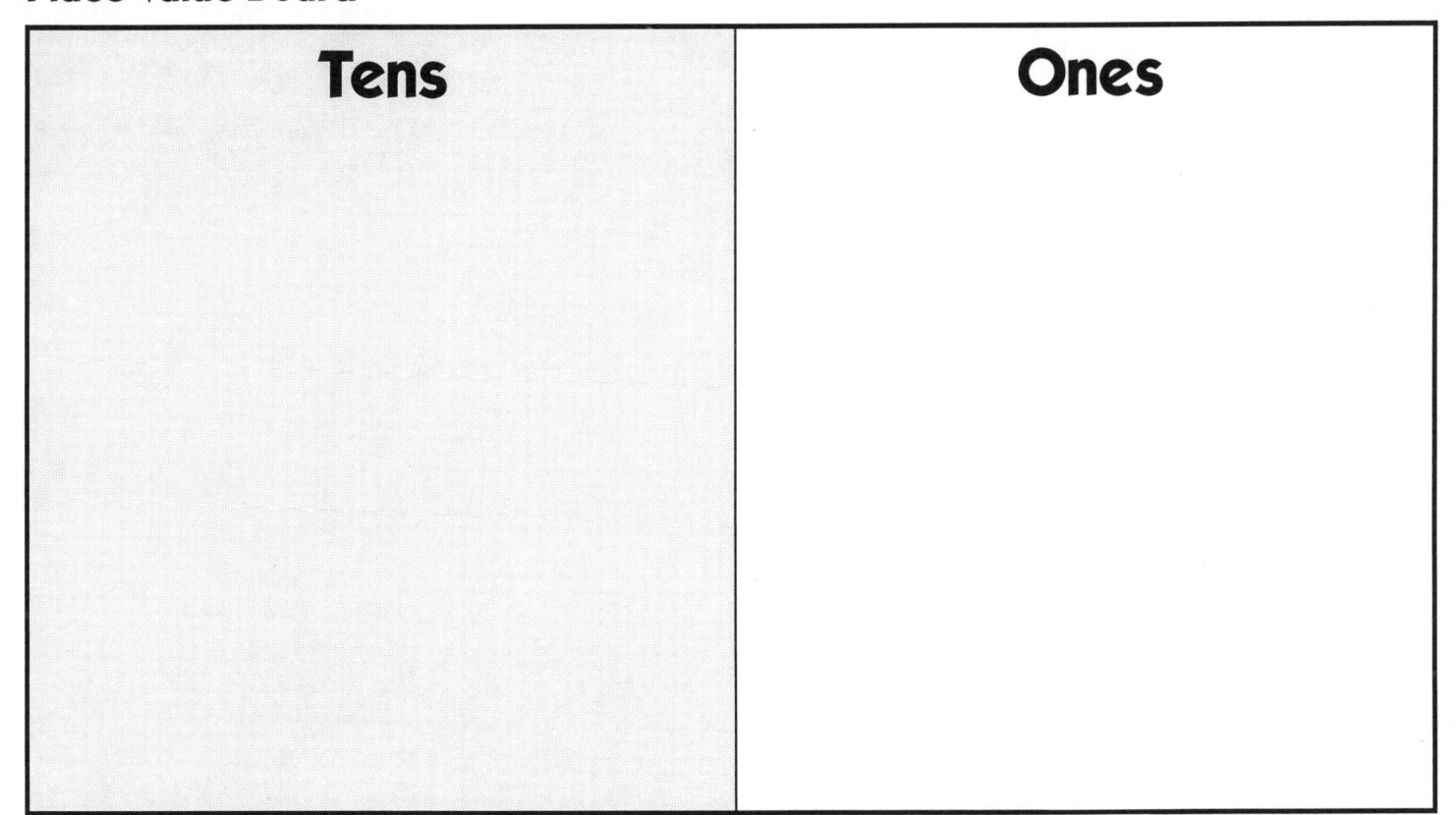

Tens	Ones